Star Apocrypha

Star Apocrypha

Christopher Buckley

TRIQUARTERLY BOOKS
NORTHWESTERN UNIVERSITY PRESS

EVANSTON, ILLINOIS

TriQuarterly Books
Northwestern University Press
Evanston, Illinois 60208-4210

Printed in the United States of America
10 9 8 7 6 5 4 3 2 1

ISBN 0-8101-5128-6 (cloth)
ISBN 0-8101-5113-8 (paper)

Library of Congress Cataloging-in-Publication Data

Buckley, Christopher, 1948–
Star apocrypha / Christopher Buckley.
p. cm.
ISBN 0-8101-5128-6 (cloth : alk. paper) —
ISBN 0-8101-5113-8 (paper : alk. paper)
1. Philosophy—Poetry. 2. Metaphysics—Poetry. I. Title.
PS3552.U339 S73 2001
811'.54 — dc21
2001000128

The paper used in this publication meets the minimum requirements of the American National Standard for Information Sciences—Permanence of Paper for Printed Library Materials, ANSI Z39.48-1984.

We were the uncountable stars, at first.
We were nothing at first, and the light
of what was already over still in it.
—*Larry Levis*

Contents

III

Acknowledgments

Special thanks to the editors of *Passager* for selecting "Zeno Said" as the winning poem in its 1998 poetry contest.

American Poetry Review "Keeping My Own Company"
Colorado Review "Star Apocrypha"
Crazyhorse "Eclipse"
The Hudson Review "Observation: Middle Age"
The Journal "Some Last Existential Thoughts at Surf Beach," "Winter Residue"
Mid-American Review "Photograph of Myself"
The Montserrat Review "*Allegro Non Troppo*"
Passager "Zeno Said"
Quarterly West "Road to Damascus," "Early Cosmology," "Apologia: The Bible-History Student Returns Home," "Watchful"
Rattle "After a Reading, Charles Bukowski Returns & Gives Me the Lowdown on Fame, Mutability, the Afterlife, et al. . . . ," "March 21, & Spring Begins on Benito Juarez's Birthday in Mexico"
SOLO "Prayer to Escape the East," "Via Dolorosa"
Third Coast "Phlogiston Theory & the Clouds of the Old World," "Lost Sky"
TriQuarterly "Metaphysical Trees"
Whirligig "Last Days of the Hot-Rod Kids"

Special thanks for editing help and suggestions, friendship, and support to Gary Young, Jon Veinberg, Gary Soto, and Nadya Brown.

I

Keeping My Own Company

quien habla solo espera hablar a Dios un dia
—Antonio Machado

After all, the afternoons are off gossiping among the pines,
and the first excursions

of stars won't start up south of here for an hour, climbing
that bright net, and there

at the far end of evening, beyond the dim light of the patio,
they will again confirm nothing

so absolute as the inattentive moon. Closer to home, jays
annotate the doubtful margins

of the oaks, and a mockingbird tells all he's learned from
trial and error—little more

than a coating of dusk on his wings to show for it. Otherwise,
I have only met up with middle age,

a man in shirt sleeves walking away, across the ruined fields,
a man who, without noticing,

crosses over to another country where the roadside grasses are still
burning at his heels, where

the same clouds clang overhead, and that ache in his back—dull
as those tin clouds—says only

that the dark is coming on. It seems improbable that more might be
revealed on a day no different

than the rest, when I have again gone dreaming the roads of my youth
with their white discouraged dust,

alongside olive and lemon groves, with roses burning beneath the sun,
a fragrance of sorrow on the air.

And so I also miss the Milky Way, the swirled spangle and milt,
all the misplaced evidence of God

swimming away. Who am I talking to each evening across the table,
the candle wavering between us?

A boy with a satchel of stolen tangerines, a man sporting that
dust-colored houndstooth coat

from the Thrift? Lord of the warblers, Lord of ice in the heart
of the red-shouldered hawk,

Lord of dust that has settled all week in the glasses for wine, today
I desire nothing from the world.

Here I am, the same so far, heart like a weed holding on, the globe
hardly moving. And it comes to me

that I was never meant to interpret the heavens, meant for nothing
more than the minor admonishments

of wind, a scoured sky responding to the last blue petitions
                                        of the sea, where I wish again

for a little space to breathe, where I am taken with the spindrift,
                                        the implicit small talk of stars.

Apologia: The Bible-History Student Returns Home

SANTA BARBARA, CALIFORNIA

White clouds pass high above the invisible
pillared sky, as if they'd somehow forgotten

everything. Yet I recall Xerxes and Darius Mede,
heavy iron the Hittites bore, the dangling horticultures
of Babylon which aren't even sand any more. . . .

Only up the coast in Guadalupe and the Nipomo Dunes,
The Ten Commandments was shot by Cecil B. de Mille,

who abandoned the obelisks and cement Sphinx,
the high parapets of Egypt, to the sea of 1923,
to the sands shifting anonymously as any distance in Assyria.

Sweet Jesus, we then went door-to-door in our cloud-white
parochial shirts, in the blood of the lamb, hawking booklets

of Holy Seals to be rewarded with the plastic bodies of saints
glowing in the dark, who looked nothing like the photos
of bony, balloon-bellied Pagan Babies the archdiocese

pinned to classroom walls, the better to drive us out
into the streets collecting more. For every twenty dollars

we named a child, and sent those poor souls forth
beneath the ungodly weight of *Constantine* or *Charlemagne*,
anointed for the vainglorious world of 1958.

But weekends free among the hills, unreformed at heart,
I was fearless of the perpetual fires, for there was no

angel's blood on the lintel of the air, no sign above
the thin, indefinite music of the sea my lack of faith
revealing only that dry leaves scattered in my hands

like old light, like sand. I heard no voices falling
from the scaffolding of wind as I shot through my thirties

like a bottle rocket fizzing into the blank reaches of noon
until one March along the shore—wearing my Chinese cap,
same ivory scarf against the salt wind at our throats—

he looked right through me, a rind of sun humming
above his head. A gust came up, spun me around

with bits of seaweed flagging the air; a veil of sand,
and I could swear finally only to a chalk-colored silhouette
slipping away, muffled by the sea—the fine dry silt

of contemplation come to little more than the clouds
dragging their dark anchors across the foothills of home,

suffused by the low sea-moan and limbo of the dark.
I tug my cap down against the onshore breeze,
a little salt drying on my cheek; I have returned

from my travels in the East and am halfway meek.
The birds lead silence through the air—"Midcareer"

must have come and gone—my mind like a sponge wrung out
with the watery, high apotheosis of the past,
with the lost phrasing of those stars still overhead,

the galaxies' buzzing light like bees at a spring bush. . . .
Perhaps there was something else, all this way from Nineveh.

Eclipse

This was predictable, a science
of heavenly bodies, and Sister Stella Marie
told us how Columbus, knowing
his charts and stars, astonished
the inhabitants of the New World
and saved himself and his men
saying—as the sky went black as metal
for five full minutes—he would not
return the sun. . . .
                                        And so at half past
9:00 we were marched out of arithmetic
and 1956—fractions and flash cards clustered
across our desks—and onto the playground.
Each of us had one eye closed and one brown
negative our mothers packed us off with
pressed to our other eye as the sun slid
like a dark half-dollar into the greying
envelope of the sky, an ink blot
bleeding through.
                                        The morning turned
the color of tea and poured around our
outstretched arms; I saw the yellow moon
of the tetherball turn pale as skim milk
and the shadow of the flagpole dissolve

into the asphalt. The sun burned fully black
and Sister admonished us not to look
directly at it or the fringed light of creation
would burn our eye blind.
                                        The softened
smoky air, the ghostly figures on the negatives—
a bleached tree, the first house I could remember,
my father with hair whiter than a star,
foreshadowing the ash he would become,
that we all were, there on the other side
of light—
            revolved in the dim and unfamiliar
daylight like a constellation of dust,
like talc shaken off the shoulders of an old coat
over the grey sea.
                              I watched the cold blossom
of time dissolve while the soot of light lifted
and turned finally back into high blue gauze,
the red edges of our fingers pulling
the sun back to us above the bright horizon line—
all of us there below it, shining again
for a short while, adding up like clockwork,
before the common denominator of the dark.

Early Cosmology

Where am I when I first hear the high orbiting
harmony of April Stevens and Nino Tempo's
"Deep Purple," or the Marcels' doo-wopped
"Blue Moon" nonsense circling the lyrics of love
and reverberated on KIST's Top 40?
                                                            Somewhere
unknown on night-wide State Street,
submerged in that boat of a Belair, cruising
forever on a dollar fifty's worth of gas,
tuning in each *bomp bomp-bomp-bomp,*
ba bomp ba bomp bomp, dip da dip-dip,
thinking . . . God knows what
I was thinking—the charged gloss
of streetlights rebounding off the chrome
buttons of the radio—all that electricity
spinning off into the everlasting sky.

Kathy Young & the Innocents swirled
"A Thousand Stars" through bad speakers
in a rust-bucket Chevrolet—a six-pack
in the trunk, and a misery mute enough
on the side streets as I turned up the tunes
and took in the salt air's intoxication

as if I understood the mind's invisible
source of light, and from where in the under-
elaborated heavens it was likely to break clear.

And just for the record, I never knew
Art Rimbaud and his all-star jazz quintet—
who played alto and who sipped rum
from a flask tinkling the ivories to
"I Left My Love in Babylon"—never knew who
slipped out of Toledo with guns or booze,
threw that cymbal shining like the rings
of Saturn from the window of the Merc,
the radio slurring "Stardust."

I picked it all up later with black and white
spanning the prairies; Halo shampoo
and Old Golds—a Word from Our Sponsor.
Coast to coast, Edward R. Murrow
at the center of a solar system of smoke.
Andre Kostelanetz's "Sabre Dance"
was the music of the spheres on *Ed Sullivan*
for some soul sweating it out
in a tuxedo and pencil mustache
frantically balancing dishes on sticks,
running along a table, spinning
another before the first ones
collapsed from orbit
in that starry air—Father fiddling
with the wiry arms of the antenna
when the images went ghostly.
A couple minutes of stage light
and suspended saucers were all
the black & white '50s required.

What chance now someone out there
in the unwavering wherever
will one day care to uncode our beams,
and figure where, on the background track,
among some stuttering powder-bright stanzas,
we ever were?

Each night of your remaining
few thousand nights, all those galaxies
and plasma-colored nebulae still
spinning in your head, you walk up
the dark hill from work, looking out
to the Milky Way, the hiss wobbling
in the center of the egg-yolk wheel—
and you retrace every constellation
you know, all the self-conscious metaphors
and shapes that confirm nothing more than
what a glimmering plate of dust it all might be.

Road to Damascus

Why not take some time off work, go for a spin, recall the bumper-to-
bumper satisfactions of chrome, the wide tail fins on your '59 Belair?
Here's an afternoon, as much yours as anyone's—a sky off-white as charity,
as old linen hung on a balustrade, stains of a last few clouds like tea spills,
like nostalgia, like guilt, almost rinsed away.
                                                            And that bright landscape
of the mind, gold mandala floating above the turquoise bay—the angels'
own arias skim over the arboretum. Go there. See if it does more
than waver a moment in your heart's thin air.
                                                            All this about sparrows
up early and hard at it, grateful for any opportunity, just doesn't work.
Keep the priorities in order, shoulder to the grinding wheel, eye on a star,
and see where it gets you. Eight in ten lose heart halfway to no place,
really, at all.
                        Middle age already, a draft in the wall you can't find
hitting you square between the shoulder blades. It does no good to look
for a spot dim beneath the level of the street, lit with a Hamms waterfall
or Pabst Blue Ribbon neon asking "What'll ya have?" And there order
long-neck beers while someone shoves another dime in the box and pushes
the buttons for Julius La Rosa or Vic Damone, the way the beaten fathers
of the '50s did to hang on a bit longer in comparative peace with second-rate
sentimentality on the air and cold roast beef on white as they shook their heads
which never cleared, and wondered what hit them.

My father walked out
of there long before the rest, but until the day he died got up and put on
the sport coat and tie of their kind and ran himself ragged selling
one damn thing or another—died leaving two wristwatches,
a rack of pressed slacks and tweeds, and not, as he said time and again,
one red cent.
You've looked to stars—look at the five empty points
of each hand, the rags and tail ends, the streets back there littered
with promises and lost profits, unredeemed by those easy stars
that dropped from sight as soon as work weeks lost track of themselves
in the smudged city skies. Who gave themselves unquestioningly to that
and came out the other end to the fanfare of Oldsmobiles and color TV?
More than enough if I'm any judge.
That road like any other—plenty of dust
to pass the time, and of course the dead weight of a past you can't carry
or put completely down. The days follow you out, hand on your shoulder
as you second-guess the callbacks of one crow to another along the roadside
suggesting you're off the map.
You pull over on the next rise and get out
for the sunset view—bleached light leveling the sky, the blank horizon
a paradigm past all appeal. It's only the world going up and falling back,
a fine dull talc, a little more salt worn from your skin. The wind's hand
in your pocket yet again, your cap flying off in an updraft over the cliff—
almost everything beyond reach as you stand there, waiting to see it all
suddenly radiant as never before.

Prayer to Escape the East

Ash ascending the altitudes of dawn—
and all along these tarnished clouds
have refused to accept our suffering.
Down a side street, the wind goes on
tuning its violin, a pizzicato off
the thin strings of hope, a melody
of dust.
        If you knew anything
as true as a bird's magnetic heart,
where wouldn't you be instead of here,
looking out on the blank grey measure
of another year, a street lamp
at the outpost of dusk?
                                All the old failings
circling in the moth-spattered light,
ones you've held on to so long now
they just about shine, like the sparrows
in evening's rusted trees—
                                    almost the same
birds above Rincon or Malibu, the trees
still simmering in that '60s slow

Pacific sun, the glassy waves repeating
their incomplete sentences about the present,
and the past—surfboards spiked upright
in the sand like totems for the last city
of gold.

            And looking off
in that lost direction, back that far west,
the string section in the palms picks up,
and who's that on Coast Highway 1,
blond as Tab Hunter or Sandra Dee,
pulling up to Trancas in a convertible
Chevrolet?

              If there were angels,
why would they come forward now
to acknowledge another complaint?
And what small comfort could there be
in their terribly bright memories
of everything?

                    It's the same future
waiting there regardless, unthreading
through the blue eucalyptus—your guess
as good as the birds', singing their hearts out
for nothing but the last crumbs
of daylight pinpointing the small space
of their lives.

                  What use asking what more
you could ask for. You might as well
look out there to where they said
the big picture was and watch the credits roll
before the bandages and plastic bottles arrive
on the tide

              with the grainy underbelly
of industrial light. What's left to contribute

to the dark? The echo and churn of the waves?
Only that to confirm the eternal at your back.
So why not
                pick up this dust-colored feather,
carry it to your rented room and open the glass
doors above the river, unclench your fist, and let it
float out in the first direction, as unlikely as luck.

Winter Residue

Brown shoes beaten
into submission, witnesses
to everything—yellowed rind
of light in the pocket
of my old tweed coat,
there, in the smooth inner lining
just above the heart, where the ash
of stars has been collecting
since I was 39.
                    The dead
of afternoon, and a little sun,
like old wishes, like bruised gardenias
in a bowl, filters through
the paralytic trees—
                              the white glare
off the sea speaking
in the syllogisms of salt,
that invisible distillation,
syllables and anaphora
of breath, the least that is required
in the atelier of the wind.

The liquid pattern of swifts,
their music and dark recapitulation

across the green spring air,
but now what do they, what do we,
bring to the sky?
                                        A dull speculation,
the unlikely probability of constellations,
snowflakes that never fall, bread crumbs
that never reach our hands. What more
is there left to make of things?

The boundaries of air take us
just so far—in return for nothing,
the edges of shadows, indifferent shapes
absorbed into the grey walls.
From the slope of the roofs
a low mist rolls away at dawn
and anyone can tell that
the houses are a little drunk with it all,
but by afternoon, all the past
will again be almost clear.
                                                        And down
the old halls, all we have is
the smoke from abstractions—
intellectual soot, the conditional absolutes
that pulled no one from the sea.

Yet, something of me might hover
with fog in Montecito above where
I left my blood on the asphalt
in the school yard; or on the dashboard,
something of my shouting
just before the impact and scattered glass
might be lingering over that hairpin turn
on Indio Muerto Street—steam
from the radiator gone to powder, to air,
skid marks climbing the dark. . . .

And always above Mission Canyon,
such loneliness by the yellow acacias
as we knew, the rain that fell
all through childhood. Nearby,
my white parochial shirt remains
in the air like a small cloud
bled of grace.
                    How long
has my soul been gathering wool?
O stupid clouds, O fates
among the irreconcilable
webbings of the sky—a bit
of everything floats back down to us.

Above that, enough dust to keep
the sky contrite, vaguely blue—
above that, the cold light of space.
But today, not even the bird that I hid
in this poem for later, to save us
from some least portion of remorse,
returns singing with a twig.

II

Zeno Said

At 50, up Cold Springs Trail to Montecito Peak

Zeno said—though I have this secondhand—
that I'd never make it up this path.
                                        But here I am,
more than halfway to the sky,
fixed on a point but moving forward
despite his arrow across the stadium, half
of halfway, ad infinitum.
                              So much
for theory in its thin apparel, its ready-to-wear.
So much, as well, for Someday, Maybe,
and the Sweet By-and-By.
                              Three hours to the top,
legs burning, the angst of clouds
building in my lungs.
                         I wipe sweat
from my forehead, and watch little crowns of mist
evaporate from the oaks.
                              What was I thinking?
At this point, whoever looks for signs
and wonders will never get there. Jesus,
this is just dirt, and it comes to an end.
Even a little way up you can see that

whatever the Meek will inherit,
it's not this sparkling coast, not these haciendas
brazed with jacaranda and palm.
                                        I have done the math,
the life by fractions—the heart counting its way
steadily out of the world.
                                I am unraveling
with the cowslip and morning glory,
with the star-blue ceanothus, my breath
coming short with the lisp of bay laurel and eucalyptus,
and by evening we are all unheard prayers.

Overhead, my old company of clouds, the respiration
of the dead suspended above their ardent bodies.
So much for the world,
                                I think they say.

At this height, I know the extravagance of air,
the unrestricted future falling away, the hung fire—
so much for detachment.
                                Even with the view
from the peak, what do we finally know
of ourselves, let alone the angels
who have gone about each dawn in their old coats,
a mist bright as wind through the oat straw
our only clue?
                    Only half the darkness
ever peels back from the earth,
and in these valleys and swales,
in the last shadows, you can still see that.

Now, I don't know what to ask for—
all the galaxies like nerve endings

in their bright net, pulsing,
and pulling back.
                So much for the world
where the angels have lost something too,
or fallen from faith with the indecipherable
longing that supports the heavens.
The arithmetic of stars is beyond me,
the lost chalk of saints in the sky.

That poor soul, shivering in a trench coat,
living in the rusted truck by the trailhead,
his greasy arm in a greasy sling, making his forbidden fire
of twigs, tipping his green bottle up like a trumpet,
was silent, and disappeared behind the smoke
as we passed.
            I'm sure from here
he's had a clear view to the sky each night,
to the bright mad head of the comet,
its white fizzy light like one lost wing,
like a smear of silver nitrate cauterizing the dark—
ten thousand years to the other side
and back. So much for time.
                        I doubt now
he expects much from a sky that apportioned
these various poverties here below.
                            I doubt
the abstract comforts of philosophy
have kept anything close to bitterness away.
Oh, that dream of the shadow of smoke—
so much for hope.
                It's just memory
counting back, that desire to know, finally,
what it means to be here—I mean besides everything—

and from this mountain see the earth
curve out,
                    turning over and off into space,
and space itself seem nothing more
than a white dust over the parochial sea
where we were sure of the view once, by the Aegean.

Sure, there are things you can still pray for.
The clouds offer no argument against one realm
moving invisibly and without dissent at the edge
of another,
                    persuaded by the least suggestion
of wind in the manzanita to move beyond it all.
You can pray to be a cloud, I guess—
you can be that alone.

                                        But I always hear
the voices of children in the trees,
and know there the incalculable velocity of loss,
where, above the town, I stood
in my cloud-white uniform shirt with stars
pasted on my collar, and sang songs in French
I'd learned by heart.
                                        Now, as the light falls short,
I turn west for the diminuendo of starlight
rising on the blue scales of the past,
where everything has always been
floating perilously like candles in paper sacks
sent from the creek mouth out to sea.
So much for souls.
                                        Haven't I had enough?
Not by half. Not even when I think
I've tempered grief and immediately
new points of pity fill in—hip pointer,

hamstring, bone spur, ventricular arrhythmic beat—
and I find myself settling for one dog-easy day,
just loose in the old streets on a Sunday,
ambling somewhere in the sun.
And that turns out to be no place,
finally, to recover anything—a few blocks
from the creek bed, and plastic grocery bags scuttle
through the new housing sites, one snagged
like some child's lost gown in the high, thin boughs.

Hasn't the sky put up with our nonsense
all this time? Only half defeated by gravity,
why not pour what's left of your ambition
like a tablespoon of salt into the Pacific?

The avatars and ascended masters, I'm told,
sit in the silent altitudes with little to do,
despite snow and cloud banks that occlude a world
where community leaders take up resolutions
against the enervation of the grass,
where you can almost hear the lost anthems of elms
beyond the cul-de-sac.
                                        The last mastodons
grew small and survived another twenty thousand years
on the Channel Islands. You're finally breathing
the blue pure air, crossing in the unqualified
direction of the light—so why question its glaze
igniting the date palms along the shore
like the stars that find their way
each night, clear across the sky?

Last Days of the Hot-Rod Kids

Butch Wax, Brylcreem, Wildroot Cream-Oil, and more in our hair,
Tuck Schneider, Fowler, Sozzi, and me thought we were somebody—
we whipped it into a wave that peaked and never broke—Jelly Rolls,
fenders, wings, spit-curl waterfalls in front, and Flattops,
a glimmering, Doo-Wop, quintessential sea of grease.
1950s, it was all
you had—a republic of style, marshaled with nothing more than a comb.
Freddy Canon, Fabian, and Fats Domino on record jackets, on *Bandstand,*
studio lights rebounding off their high-rolling hairstyles that had hardened
into place—Elvis, on movie posters, on TV from the waist up. And if not
them, then Tuck's big brother, Joe, home from Catholic High—blue jeans
stiff with the ¼-inch roll at the cuff, a red windbreaker Jimmy Dean wore
in the movie as a first-class juvenile delinquent. Like a Major Leaguer
stepping to the plate, Joe would stop, spread his legs, then pull a comb
from his back pocket and make long, slow passes through the wings
of his Ducktail to the point where they met in back of his head,
to the point where he was suspended from school for three days,
for such hair was dangerous stuff.
We became our own cause as Dean
flipped a cigarette from the curb and blasted off in a hot-rod Dodge.
We were hip before the bell rang for us to line up by grades, arm's distance,
facing flag and crucifix for the Pledge of Allegiance and Apostles' Creed,
and we ducked into the washroom, putting parts on the left and mowing

our front-combed tops to the side, turning our collars down so we truly
resembled the accountant's, farmer's, and Jr. Chamber of Commerce's sons
we were.

And as soon as they boarded the bus, eighth-grade girls popped
open compacts and applied lipstick—blood rose and tangerine—rolled up
their uniform skirts to just below the knee which was where the House
Un-American Activities Committee wanted to start investigating
the subversive jungle influence of rock 'n' roll. On the sidewalks after school,
they were sure they'd be taken for Judy Holiday, Gina Lolabrigida, or
Sandra Dee, as they swayed down the streets in saddle shoes, confidently
snapping their gum.

Louis De Ponce's metallic-green '58 Chevy bellowed
all 348 cubes up East Valley Road every day during study hall and told us
that soon we'd be riding our ten-speeds to Tuck's to play the latest 45s—
the Ventures, Duane Eddy, Jorgan Ingman, as much amplified Stratocastered
twang as we could get at a dollar a disc, and this would go on forever,
or for another year—

until the '60s and high school, where we were new and
no one, where class leaders were sheared by barbers who left "white sidewalls"
above their ears, where they voluntarily wore suits and ties on test days, where
nuns, priests, and Junior Achievement eliminated every black motorcycle jacket,
chrome zipper, chain, and slicked-back hairstyle from the scene. Many
sported Crew Cuts, though no one had the first idea what crew really was.
We joined Key Club, Lettermen's Club, fool-happy to set up chairs for assembly,
sell religious chocolate bars door-to-door. Despite Kennedy, Peace Corps, and
the New Frontier, Republicans were still on the corporate golf course and not
disposed to look the other way to Johnny Cool, Hey Daddy-O, low riders
in souped-up Chevys and Mercs who would never have a charge account.
No, we were all going to wear loafers, wing tips, and button-down shirts.
James Dean had been T-boned in his Porsche near Cholame and was a bit of
blond dust over Highway 41 and the past; Elvis was in the army, a buzz cut
like every other grunt.

And who knew—in their beehives and bouffants
shining like chiffon, in their stiff dresses—what mysteries girls were holding
back? If we were going to find out, going to get ahead, we had to put on

business suits, tie our thin ties through tab collars, and ask them to dance
to a band sappy with trombones, and even then some were wearing white
felt gloves to show their mothers had not forgotten the cotillion's applications
of thick grace. The chaperones scrutinized the space between us as we leaned
into each other inch by inch in the dark, and later, only a few older ones
took the path of least resistance out to the parking lot, ducking below
the dash to avoid the flashlight of the padre on patrol.

                                                                                1965 arrived, and
Orsua and I had hair to our collars and were almost expelled. Soon, half
our generation would be hated for long hair and their opposition to
the organizations of death. And though I'd studied French in school,
that was more than half my life ago, and I didn't know Dien Bien Phu
from Doo Wha Diddy, Long Binh from Long Tall Sally. I didn't know
that in no time the government would make skinheads and numskulls
out of most of us, send us to the road's end of our youth in the streets
of Berkeley, Chicago, or Saigon without regard for who we were or might
ever be—for the blood caked in body bags or in our unfashionable hair—and
so haircut or not, it looked like I was headed for Canada, and nowhere fast.

Phlogiston Theory & the Clouds of the Old World

> . . . phlogiston was the substance of fire—i.e. when an object burned, phlogiston was supposed to be given off. The remaining ash was said to be the "true" material.
>
> —*Edward McNall Burns et al.*, World Civilizations, *6th ed., vol. 2*

Something is missing, the clouds always say—
        surrounded by history and a dreary sky,
they rub the light raw until it's smudged and tarnished
        and takes on the rust or ocher hues of earth—
inamoratas of the soul, they barely resemble themselves
        occluding a corner of the blue, and are not thick enough,
not stuffed with enough high arrogance, to ask if below,
        the red and random dots of poppies have meaning.
They still carry the staffs of lightning that pierced the breast
        of St. Teresa and drove her into a closed-eye ecstasy,
where she sips at the thin air over the mountain peaks
        which portend the end of all things as we are carried off
cold, naked as light, in the dim cumulus of space. I will not be
        deceived by the music of the trees, always sourced somewhere else—
everything passing through the porous air of our own regard,
        the direction wind takes through our hands.

What happened to the Huguenots after St. Bartholomew's Day?
      Dirt happened to the Huguenots—2,000 returned to it.
In Paris that night, it did not rain, but no one was playing
      violin caprices or fandangos at court.
And the Maid of Orléans said there was something
      in the clouds, some star-white direction,
some steel-brilliant voices that did not allow the flames
      to take the stubborn muscle of her heart.
The earth still looks inescapable for all intents and purposes,
      the unrestricted future yet to be heard from
in some small places where the sky is moist, a green cloud
      rising from the forest floor where fire and iron are still
new and unquestionable. But what else might we suppose?
      How essential are we, what are we after all else fails?

Can we identify a preamble of light inside us, our own source
      we eventually all have to give up—and who are we then,
what do we have left? And who ever agreed to death?
      Crowd scenes in Dutch painting said we were happy
working ourselves steadily in that direction, come ice or fire,
      while the well-to-do in white collars looked on
from somewhere just beyond the vanishing point, content
      in their church-black outfits, and apparently no one
complained about the storm clouds roiling above the hay bales,
      driving in, the horses going wild with the lightning strikes,
or the stars frozen in the rivers that were dying and we could not see,
      that we skated over the entire fifteenth century.

So we were tossed a metaphysical bone, an afterlife, a shimmering
      soulful concourse of ether, another loose assembly
of clouds, another pale day limping along, building and dissolving
      exactly the way the nineteenth century did, shuffling across
the English midlands in galvanized striations where Charlotte Brontë
      and her sisters religiously wrote them down, and died
drinking the water that seeped downhill from the cemetery,
      from the dulled atmosphere—the clouds low and scumbled,

rubbing the names on the limestone markers away.
    And with Constable, the spiraled, cathedral shine, clouds
milky and glazed with a grey that always promised rain,
    which kept you pinned to earth beneath their wing-
spread and immaculate regalia of grief, bruise-blue
    at evening's edge, like a gas flame cut back.

But how bright I was in social studies that grey day,
    gazing out the window to nothing but clouds gathering,
my mind half a cloud then when I managed to stand
    and clearly answer *Antoine Lavoisier*
when called on—one of the fathers of modern chemistry
    our chapter said, who, in the late 1700s,
invented an apparatus for the decomposition of air,
    who named oxygen and hydrogen, gave us the molecular
equation for clouds, and delivered the final blow to
    the Phlogiston Theory, proving that while matter
may change forms, it's never destroyed, which reassured me
    then that we were what we were, no matter what.
Sitting down in my desk—having done my homework that time
    so I might say *Antoine Lavoisier* in my best French accent—
I drifted back out the window where the sea-colored olive trees
    bent a little with wind and snapped back to form.

And now all this light later, gone God knows where, I'm left
    with my father still singing "I Cover the Waterfront."
He glides along in his Pontiac, fifty years ago on Cabrillo Boulevard—
    the street lamps with their tear-drop glass and green light
coming on, dotting the powdered-blue backdrop of evening,
    the tangerine-edged bouquets of clouds above the sea,
passing over all that still life, as if it would never burn out.

After a Reading, Charles Bukowski Returns & Gives Me the Lowdown on Fame, Mutability, the Afterlife, et al. . . .

I'm not even drunk!—we both say that as, ship size and grey, he floats in. . . . I'm on the second floor overlooking the motel's postage-stamp pool. The TV's turned itself off, and I've drifted in and out of the hot arms of a Santa Ana wind, door open to the background tracts of ocean and boulevard.

His face is still rough as a potato, and right off he tells me to open us a Bud, and light up one of those knock-off Hondurans—even the smoke and ash of this life are still beautiful, he says. Set that bottle over here by the window where I can remember it, you don't need another one—tomorrow, no one will care who didn't show up.

Hell, I'm gone five years and I'm still publishing more than you—the books just keep coming like horses rounding the turn at Santa Anita. Life's not fair—but death's no nap in the park. Listen pal, I had a huge backlog, one publisher, and no awards—I didn't gripe, and I never did drink as much as I used to.

You'd better just keep up with your typing—you're not young enough to complain anymore. The days run away like, well you should know that one at least—like taxis at rush hour in New York, let's say, but I can't help you there. You've been out of the friends-and-glory loop since the get-go. You don't really want to be one of those three- or four-book Selected Poem types—then what's left? Look, there's nothing they haven't already not given you that they can't give you anymore—you're bulletproof. Have another on me, but spare me the rhymers and one more villanelle—Jesus, just remember who you are, those holes in your sneakers in grammar school, and write something someone will want to read before they die.

Besides, there's no one over here in a monkey suit passing around silver trays of sandwiches with the crusts cut off and a pitcher of Manhattans, little envelopes with awards from the Academy. Nothing really changes. Someone goes around with star dust and famous sport coats, all fitted out before you arrive. You have to be in line with the forty-dollar haircut and a handsome mug. Christ, you might even have to have a theory. It's tough all over

All that stuff happens over a famous lunch—it's just the arithmetic of fate, like comets rolling up more ice and dust, or a sandwich wrapper on the sidewalk gathering more flies. Yeah, I read about that Prix de Rome, guys in pressed pants walking the Via del Corso praising the pines, memorizing names of Italian aperitifs when there's perfectly good beer—all on the government. It's nice work, but you're not in the club.

I voted for the Prix de L.A., a tab at the Pantry—a porterhouse steak and potatoes au gratin—but the phone never rang. Something like that little Argentinean grocery in Glendale with the pungent sausage, spinach pie, a jolt of yerba maté. What you live for every day. Stay home and work with that. Even a crude bastard like me still knows the real music of the world hanging above the avenues. Hell, I even loved German opera—any chump in a cheap restaurant knows Italian, but Jesus, that might be what love is? I know, I know, you think I should have a handle on that one by now, but I'm only dead, not enlightened.

As far as I can see, the freeways are well lit, and hazy or not, light is light and it falls gloriously every day somewhere in the world, like butter melting on rye toast—just don't flinch and praise some jerk's bad poems to get in one of those anthologies, or to catch a ride in his Lexus to some celebrity party at a swank place in the hills, and some of it will get to you. Cities of light, lots of light—everything radiant as hell. But where does that leave you?

If you're like me, it leaves you still dreaming about a small fishing village on the east side of Baja, a place where no one expected anything of you beyond a sloppy rendition of "Cielito Lindo" in the cantina on Saturday night—a place 20 years ago when even a measly royalty check bought you a thatched cabana and peace, shrimp the size of your fist, and the empty bay of Cortez was as far as rewards went on earth, each sunset the fish jumping blue and silver from the unappreciated beer-gold sea.

Some Last Existential Thoughts at Surf Beach

LOMPOC, CALIFORNIA

Who hasn't looked at the sea
and seen our position here
as untenable as the snowy plovers'
who congregate like theologians
along the tide line and scatter
as the simple dark comes on?

Sand dollars like broken alphabets
scar the beach, ineffable, old
as complaint.
                    Unlike the plovers skirting
the edges, their windup legs racing
for all they're worth up and back
with the incoming tides, it only matters
now that we're direct, that the soul,
with all it's held back, is loosened
simply as the light from stars.
                                        I make do
with evening's tree-wrapped stars
which have always lent themselves

to the case made for detachment
or which have more or less
spelled out whatever it was
I thought I wanted—though stars
finally are still so bourgeois.

And while the casual attributes of light
can't be the whole thing, and I have
continually looked out to stars—this deep
blue is all I've really had, sea or sky,
simple anodyne for the dark, and
the rock-obvious fact of the world.

I don't think Jean-Paul Sartre worried
about transcendence, but about
the chicken Simone de Beauvoir liberated
from back of the butcher's during the war—
half rotten and curried and served for dinner—
and about his first play, sweated out
in a German POW camp on scraps of paper,
the long months of clouds going over
suggesting what probably didn't matter.

I drive by the broccoli fields on Sundays,
evenings, and rainy days, and the Mexican workers
in baseball caps and yellow slickers
are shouldering irrigation pipe, bending
with hoes.
            They have an idea
about what amounts to something in the world,
and in Wal*Mart pay cash for jeans and motor oil
and with the sun dying in the dirt
have no thoughts for New Historicism,
the perplexed heart of Albert Camus,
the academic elaboration of grief.

Sartre survived admiring the lunettes
in the high ceiling of the Grand Hotel
Quel Que Chose; Simone de Beauvior despaired
of cooking anything and they went out
each evening for drinks at Left Bank bistros,
late dinner at a brasserie—streetlights
and stars on the river, the *bateau mouche*
moving slowly as fate into the dark—and so
put up with each other's assignations, writing
home half sadly, lighting up Gauloises,
and letting the smoke drift off
with the life of the mind.

My friend Peter once told me
I was the oldest young man he knew—
I was a young man for so long,
and whatever I believed before, I believed it—
now, for the life of me, it's so dim
back there that I don't know what.

Walking through the old town,
I've seen Death ride past
the thrift stores on a Mexican bicycle,
in white washboard bones, ringing his little bell
through the metaphysical afternoons.

And now I think I've seen Machado's shepherds
in their autumn-colored capes, traipsing home
over the foothills, through the orange and avocado groves
which give off, in winter, a little violet smoke
that covers the tiny music of their herds. . . .

Agnus Dei, how I always want to know
the trees, their green sweep across the air,
and the wind's coloratura underscoring

the birds flying slowly into the sky. . . .
Dear God, don't answer me now,
don't answer at all.

March 21, & Spring Begins on Benito Juarez's Birthday in Mexico

In Mexico today, Benito, you are 193
springs beyond the sun—and in the village
of Ixtlan, there are no Zapotecs
left to remember.
                    You are on my calendar
here in California, and this morning
there is the tablecloth with the crumbs
of despair left over from every democratic thing. . . .

Thank goodness the mockingbirds are starting up,
I had almost forgotten what world
I was living in—
                    I turn from my desk to their dither,
their desires and grievances boiling up
with a new regime of light,
                                    and I can almost
see the first golden streams of monarchs lifting
from the conifers of Michoacán,
                                        their hearts
no heavier than mist releasing to the sun
as they guide back north through the industrial clouds,
past the loggers in complicity with the standard
corporations of death.

Once, Benito, the trees pointed
the way and the stars fluttered above us like
Platonic ideals—
I too gave assent to them
and everything larger than ourselves, but for days
I've been looking over the shoulder of dust—
which is everything that became of land reform—
and at times like these,
the council of the wind
proves useless.
If I have a soul, it's lost
inside my shirt—I always expected more
of my blood,
which still sings of the sea,
the chorus of salt—but like the monarchs,
we are not even the dust we leave behind.

I deliver my petitions to the waves
and receive the recapitulation of loss,
which is the old response—the shells,
the seaweed, washing in with their worth.
There is no remedy in the maps of the sky;
the civic documents pile up against the poor.

I can propose anything on this bright new air,
but I won't hold my breath,
given the spindrift, the equivocations of light.
I no longer have a child's heart—
despite sea water in every cell,
the crystals of desire, the corollary
of the stars—their threads evaporating
for centuries on the surface
and representing nothing.
I resign
my failed scholarship, my love
of the stars. I make my interpretations

of the lemon and eucalyptus leaves—
I hide whatever belongings I have left
from the sky.
                    President, old governor,
compadre in dust, all the theories fail—
it's only this ordinary bird who is bothered
finally, who still carries forward our demands.
From several possibilities each morning
we will reach for hope, every time, on the branch
of hopeless things.
                         Today, in our bare feet,
this new season is everything that's sure
on earth, the earth that will never be divided
equally among any of us—
                                   at best,
and at long last, we drift through the air
no more than the dreams from trees.

Star Apocrypha

Where stars are concerned, I am as enthusiastic
as the next one—those planets just forming

across the cosmic lot, the cold blue quasars finally
arriving after fifteen billion years,

one apparently as hopeful as the next. I think we all
came to live in this world so why

should the sea in its white glitter, fasting for the sun,
or the stutter in a line of clouds have us

thinking of death, the continuing resolution of the dark
that reads entirely across the sky? For exuberance

we have the shoal of stars, the command performance
and grand galactic archipelagoes, the sea foam

and abacus of stars. Yet all the time, finite by definition—
they have done the math. On a smaller scale,

I can no longer enjoy even a small espresso without
considering the atomic consequences—

arrhythmia, free radicals, and pancreatic dissolution, but
there are other examples—St. Catherine of Siena

living for years on nothing but the host of air, levitating
as purely as the stubborn light she was becoming.

Why then be on earth? Yet even I fly through the blue night
sometimes, in my astral body, light as the bread

she would not eat, and for a while there, above the palm trees
and cypresses, all things seem possible to a man,

who, though he knows his weight on earth, can, among his friends,
lift off the sidewalk, rise to the occasion of wind,

of his improbable dreaming soul, as it floats away, effortless
in its modesty, in his star-white shirt—and godwit

or sanderling, be as congenial, as satisfied to receive the sun
off the spume of waves, the gilded aura of thought

lifting from the star pine's boughs, the small contributions
to the infinite panoply, the boundless savor of light. . . .

The dove who arrives on my balcony, and paces the railing
in her flame-colored feet, is not a poetic truth,

but an earthly one who stands for her grey apprehensive self,
dark unmetaphorical eye eyeing me

before she flutters off into the half-mystical eucalyptus
that this morning is separating wind from wind

to no avail, and which, along with the doves, seems to
repeat the long Aramaic vowels of the Essenes

swirled through canyons of the Dead Sea, almost as old as sand.
    I decipher nothing and, unlike them, I give up little,

and for lasting imperfection turn to the waves, as close to
    the scroll of stars, as beyond time, as we're going to get.

Today, what more shall we believe about ourselves? Half the time
    the stars go missing. Eye of the dove, dark as the unlocked

heart of space, there must be something else. . . . Starry needles
    just sew and unsew the dark so that the days return—

how long has the sky been waiting for all of this to arrive?
    All we are is respiration—no distance and little wind,

a verse which could quit any time—*et cum spiritu tuo*—
    the last breath gone out with the wild idea of us.

III

Photograph of Myself

MONASTERY OF MONTE TORO, MENORCA, ELEVATION 1,162 FEET

For Nadya

God almighty, I'm almost halfway glorious in this
gold houndstooth coat from the local Thrift,

all my sins left behind—you can tell by the way
so much light has gathered to reflect off the crown
of my head, shining white as that angel's gown

in the high glazed sky behind me, as if I too were called
into this life, stripped of grief and God's detachment.

Twenty years, and I'm mildly ecstatic, on sabbatical at last,
slow as a sleepwalker down any dream-bright road
that will happily have him, that will offer the dispensation
of the sun, a redemption of poppies and marguerites. . . .

Even after all the bad blood of childhood washed down
the Catholic aisles, it's fine to be here, on the sacred top

of this world, where Benedictines maintain the Blessed Mother
gave them a sign to build—the Bull of Faith in an aureate cloud
atop this table of rock. I'm just breathing the beatific air

of pines, and what interests me is the mezzanine of clouds,
the level of the sky that strains the daylight down walls

the color of clouds, and at the entrance to the parking lot
the statue of Christ raising his arms toward heaven,
or Ibiza, and that satellite dish with its red
lightning bolt of the old gods defunct behind him,

and the burnt-out tower of the TV station
which appropriated this spot closest to the sky.

Below, tides all around this rock, and each salt parable
of the sea turning like mist toward light, the Spanish
circumstance of pain to an arduous life—the procession

of penitents, ladies with bad knees and good leather shoes,
walking the tortured curves of asphalt to the top.

I ascended by car, my life lifted awhile from the world
of the faithless—I came for the view end to end
of the island, for the picnic benches under the trees,
and standing in the parking lot before the ash-white

parapets of faith, wondered if flowerlike I might turn
back a little to belief, or at least to the joy in the pale music

of the skies. In this snapshot, I could be anyone
playing it safe on Sunday—God off beyond these clouds—
indifferent enough finally that I am almost smiling,

unbothered for the first time in years. I have left
my sword and shield on the empty shore, and the truth is

I want to go no higher than the immediate deliverance
of pines and picnic tables along this ledge from where
I can see, faintly to the west, the high cliffs of Mallorca,
the business of the world held off behind a mist.

I praise the fresh bread and semi-*curado* cheese
with its dram of ewe's milk, the tart acceptable wine

from Peñedes, the dead lunch meats we've brought along
at some sacrifice to celebrate ourselves. I praise the birds
who continue to bribe the air with song—I hold my heart

out to the wind, open collared, in my ragged coat, and
want everything, at 48, still left to me under the sky.

Observation: Middle Age

CALA PADERA, MENORCA

The windfall figs fill out, wedged into the limestone cliffs,
fed on air, a bit of mist. They're good for the indeterminate
industries of ants, or a few sticks' worth of shade which fall
to the cove below where tourists and locals alike crowd
the fifty yards of sand, but do not take to the water, green
and glassy as a cat's eye. They prefer the buttery heat,
women topless in the sunny custom here; the natives are
an even nut brown, Brits and Germans paper white
and sizzling pink, all nonetheless equally acknowledged
by the light—nipples dark magenta as the ripest figs
weighing a bough, or fresh red as raspberries over cream.
I watch the lean husbands stretch and flounce, canvassing
left and right. But where does it get you looking at the lustrous
young or those edging past middle age, sitting as I am in
between, applying my sunblock in the shade? It only weighs
the heart, one more chalky stone about to tumble down
these cliffs. So I wade out alone, flip onto my back, and float
toward the deeper blue from where I still see the women
lounging beside the rocks, shaking out their blond or auburn hair,
combing it down their breasts, sun ripe and fragrant with creams
or oils. I stare up after a sail-shaped cloud, and though sea water
fills my ears, I hear the uneasy music of the waves pulled
into shore where I have abandoned every thought of home.

Watchful

ES CASTELL, MENORCA

> But the truth is that we are always watchful,
> lying in wait for ourselves. . . .
> —*Pablo Neruda*

I remember the idiot in the town square
of Es Castell, trying each day to entice
the resident pigeons to eat the orange peels
he threw blissfully, and with hope,
onto the grass and walks.
                                        But, after so much time,
they were on to him, and the worthless peels,
and waddled away in a mumbling cloud
of feathers. . . . And each day he'd finally tire
of their truculence and unzip the jacket
of his purple warm-up suit, spread it wide
as a red kite's wings, and run
into their grey midst, scattering them
a few feet beyond the fountains, but never out
above the sky-colored water,
or into the water-colored sky. . . .

Like the old men already sitting there
in the wet shadows on the benches,

we soon tolerated him—like the pigeons
who came back in a minute or two
and who seemed to forget,
as he did, such purposeless and
momentary confrontations—days
like lost clouds.
                    I soon realized
that I was blessed simply
to walk out each morning
around the square and hear
the clock tower above the post office
strike the hour two times,
a few minutes apart, and not care
which could be correct; blessed
to sit next to the public phones,
which occasionally rang for no one,
and watch the bees dissolve into the sun
with the mathematics of light—
the stars never showing any sign
of distress.
                Yet, if there is some great truth
about us, it's not in the stars,
or in the cluster of orange peels
almost as brilliant on the midmorning walk—
but perhaps in the fact that we can tolerate
one among us to whom they are of equal
consequence.
                    I no longer need to look
to stars, the poorly punctuated dark,
for no matter what I tap out on the Olivetti,
the earth still looks inescapable from here.

But if some innocence remains,
a little of it might be here
on this small island
deserted in winter by tourists,

foreign commerce, and even the attention
of the more fashionable birds.
The green finch and the swifts are
content and have their say.
The boats are in each afternoon,
gulls climbing the air after them,
praising the fruits of the sea.

And if now we are not sure
what is of value—looking out
at the fig trees thin as refugees
along the cliff—we at least understand
what is worthless before our eyes
morning after morning, as the steam
and fog of industry lift off
beyond the port and to the west
without us.
                    I sit above the harbor,
happily on the benches provided
by the *ayuntamiento* for just this purpose,
beneath the orderly palms,
freighters and cruise ships slipping
in and out, going somewhere . . .
and make do with the intuition of wind,
the pines with their impromptu rhythms,
my hands and feet free
to defeat the intricate purposes of air,
to do nothing more than claim
the prosperity of light.
                                        Late afternoon,
I like the white tables fronting
the bars in the square, relaxing
with a small *Estrella*—a beer
named for a star—knowing that,
soon enough, around the corner,
I'll be on my way back

from the market and bakery
with a heart as full as the summer
5:00 sun, with a yellow grocery bag
in each hand as I ascend the steps
to our flat over the cove, where
I'll look out, and see in the reflection
of the glass doors, a happy man
arranging oranges in a bowl.

Lost Sky

MAHON, MENORCA

100 miles in any direction and
the sky still has plenty of time,
and so is in no hurry to remember,
offer a clue
as to which life this is—
sauntering along

in a fine straw hat, summer trousers, and shirt
the color of stones lining the cart-wide streets,
anonymous against the faded building sides,

where the canaries and finches—set out
in their twig cages for the sun—and I
whistle pieces
of an aria beneath the unencumbered roofs,

thinking perhaps in terms of the heart,
of stones absolved by the sea. . . .

Winter is hardly anything
here, a white
midday moon, a sliver of ice on the blue

is as close as it comes—
a wind
is serious every so often,
the hills shrug
their shoulders beneath their old coats
of chamomile and fennel,
each morning a mist
of acquiescence lifting out to sea. . . .
And soon
the green shutters will close after the lunch hour,
late,
and there, where a bright breeze breaks
off the bay
igniting the high garden wall,
you turn once more to praise the loquats and gold
hibiscus,
hands over your eyes like a prisoner
just released into the blinding light of noon. . . .

But now the linnets have abandoned the leafless
civic trees, their branches
pointing every
which way above the horizon.
4:00, the city dead
asleep, and you find yourself at the tables
in front of the American Bar,
waiting reasonably,
as is the custom, for the waiter on duty
to stub his cigarette and set,
reluctantly,
next to your folded *Herald Tribune*,
a glass of fino, as thinly amber
as the coattails of daylight
trailing over the roof tiles
to the west,
where, for a minute or two, all the old

theologies circle,
like pigeons, like rings
of the elect, to the sky—
like the remedies of dust,
dispensed each day
at this time from the stuffed pockets
of the ragman,
shuffling alley to street, a man
of apparent contentment, who smiles and tips
his sun-bleached captain's hat
each time
he sees you, God-knows-what in the sacks
on his creaking cart.
You have half a dozen phrases
to fall back on—
one for him in the afternoon,
and one for the newsstand,
tabacalera, fish market,
and the bar—
one for the past you say to no one,
but that old high Latin
will get you nowhere now—

not comfortably back down the burning
road to home,
or to Augustine's City of God, and who

would you recognize there,
though you speak,
beneath your breath to someone
beyond the shops,
someone not among the shopping crowds
soon drifting down the streets?
At 5:00 as the lights
snap on
across from you, only the usual

ghosts of the evening hour return—
sparrows the color
of October, chorusing in praise
of the constellations,
the offerings of crumbs
wind-blown on the chairs
and ground . . .
and in the pines at sunset,
that region
of memory
dimming once again with a longing
for something
as indeterminate as the latticework of clouds,
a plume
of black smoke dissolving
into the last striations
of the blue,
as it exhales through your bones and skin
and you begin again
the little poem of the soul, recalling the lines
for the spirit
at last content somewhere, floating
through the streets
aimed no higher finally than the sugared light,
sparkling
in the bakery windows—
steam,
bright thread rising,
unraveling
through the increasingly familiar dark.

Allegro Non Troppo

Solo el silencio y Dios cantan sin fin.
—Antonio Machado

No matter
how often I sit on this bench, available
to the sky, I do not hear the angels
sing as they attend to the profligacy
of stars . . . and by any comparison,
of course, I have failed.
Silence
for my small part before the sea—
glossing the auburn hills, the bleached plumes
of pampas grass articulating each vowel of light,
the fog bank drifting in like a boy
late for supper.
30 years, and still
the poem dreamed back there—
lean and smooth as lemon wood,
bright as the star-white blossoms resonant
beyond the dark—has not appeared.
But what
longing then would fill October afternoons?
It would be all up with me, already,
no matter how rich the sunlight coming
to rest briefly in my hands.

Voices
of children rising from the beach,
all the small notes carried off bluely
into space.
I praise the elementary
rondos of my breath, the grace left
to the field larks petitioning the dusk
before December, and the dull timpani
of rain.
And for this I have no idea
what the Chinese always say—so many leaves
have fallen, the diminuendo of the blood—
and hope, an adagio of clouds . . .
time signatures at each edge of the sky.

Metaphysical Trees

> I still had two friends, but they were trees.
> —*Larry Levis*

> I went out into the woods today, and it made me feel,
> you know, sort of religious.
> —*William Matthews*

I'd like to have a eucalyptus,
a pale and slender one bouncing its loose thoughts
off the blue—
                    and maybe an avocado
with boughs like an anaconda,

and one expansive sycamore reaching out
for everything.
                    Yes, and a jacaranda,
its violet shade each June edging
the eternal past . . .
                              and a pomegranate,
I want a pomegranate with Spanish flame-
red blossoms dazzling as all get-out
in dim December.
                              While I'm at it,
I'll have an acacia, and a few Russian olives—

their aquamarine leaves recalling, of course,
the implacable sea.
                                        And a podocarpus,
those leaves Leonardo invented
to dovetail with the bronze cloud of light
backing up the Renaissance.
                                                        And all this
in a little valley arrived at through mustard weed
and fennel, white and lavender blooms of wild radish
recalling the loosely affiliated clouds,
the preliminary stars. . . .

                                                    We stepped down
from that quantum shine
                                                    clueless as to how
our bodies might be simply pronouns,
                                                                        how we stood for—
part and particle—those astral antecedents.
Right off, looking up,
                                               comparing ourselves
to the lustrous night, we complained
                                                                     of our unadorned
surroundings;
                              we would have towers,
would crawl back up the stellar imbrications
despite a prohibited tree
                                                   and all the knowledge
we would assume,
                                       despite the gardens
of Nebuchadnezzar and Assurbanipal where
the dim substance of the soul was
                                                                elucidated
against the incomparable chastity
                                                              of the sky.

And though Socrates tells us that we can learn
nothing from trees—
only from the moral man—
what about steadfastness, fortitude, perseverance,
loyalty, tenacity, not to mention
modesty, grace,
their spiritual arms,
and a dozen other abstractions
for which men die miserably?

Still, we are not that bad off
if we can get out
one afternoon and find a faithful conifer
or two to praise,
or can let the lacy shag of a pimiento
sort out the sun,
or especially if we can recall
the arboretum of childhood
and keep the camphor trees,
the pittosporum hedge, in perspective
against the vanishing point
on the air. . . .

But something was kept from us,
held over our heads, it seems, ever since—
incantations,
the chalk and diagrams of constellations
blowing by

until Latin phrases for all we were sure about
in the firmament
were inscribed in stone over
the cathedral doors and
set down darkly in orthodox

movable type,
and the world divided, and so many
taking refuge for ages in the woods. . . .

Nevertheless, as we come over the dark plateau,
there is our old town
spinning alone in light,
blister of a moon
against midnight, white static
of starlight across the desert, the salt coming
to the surface,
the ice caps evaporating,
and it's November
in Palm Springs, where I go walking in the morning
to uncloud my heart,
to keep its tumbling,
rootlike
chemistry clear,
to see four wild parrots fly
from palm to palm
as I pass the convention center,
the steamy perfume of stalks and delphiniums

rising from the moist beds
and I am 7 or 8 again
wearing a red bow tie and stiff blue
business suit
for Easter,
the glory
of the manifest world
arranged in sunlight.
Above me, the mimosa and lemon boughs,
and no text beyond that—
I mean we're protected
from the vast void of space
by nothing more than air,

and when the night calms
down to darkness
we listen
for the planets whirling by
and it's only the trees
giving us back our breath. . . .

I take those wild parrots, brilliant and green
as Eden,
as a sign from God,
admittedly
a God largely uninterested, unsure perhaps
of what more
we could possibly want—
magnolia, banyan, yew?

Maybe an indifferent sign,
indecipherable,
inadvertent,
but there are at least these four green clues
to some happiness beneath the sky. . . .

If I can't have trees, then perhaps someday just
a few yards of dirt
some fennel bushes and nasturtiums—

that portion of childhood still volunteering from the roadside,
beckoning in the winds of traffic.
For the time being
I'll take these parrots appropriating
the tops of the royal palms
as if everything were still ours
equally before the sun.

Take what you can,
you know what God will do—

he will let the complaints rise
                                        like a little smoke
dissolving against the dawn,
                                      he will turn away,
thinking perhaps
                        of another universe.

The oceans will warm
                              and drive the sailfish north,
the last log
              will be rolled out of the Amazon—
it will all go
               to hell
                     in a corporate handbasket
as we're tipping the brim of our hat
                                              over our eyes,
nodding out on the bench
                                  in the blue
absolution of shade,
                           beneath the last trees
of our forgiveness.

Via Dolorosa

SANTA BARBARA, CALIFORNIA

In those days there was more rain,
and though I stood often,
and very still, in the afternoons,
among the orange or lemon groves—
sun arriving, blooming in the water
beads on the deep waxy leaves—
no branches, in time, grew
from my arms, no blossoms
from my eyes so that I might
finally go back into the world
brilliant beyond longing.
I was transcendent only
until the dark came on
and the petitions of quail and towhees
quit along the lanes.

What it was I was forever
going to remember, I don't now know—
I went from one illuminated bough
to the next, to the sea bluff and
the Morse Code of clouds
as it revealed the vague intentions
in back of air.

How will I ever know
again but to go half lost along
that road of losses—milk-white
heart, cup of thorns, mind
of blue fragments floating off
somewhere in search of the invisible. . . .

Out the one street, headed anywhere,
we drove after school in that
beaten bronze-and-beige Chevrolet,
past the dirt road and the hand-lettered
board saying BAM'S AUTO COURT
with its half dozen trailers edging
the avocado trees, past the little
front-street grammar school
and the Rexall Drug, long past the last dairy
and lemon grove that became the first
shopping mall and so said so long
to the '60s.
There was no allegory
in the wind. The past just blew away.
We all remember some different part
of the dust blowing up from a side street
and catching in the air as we let out
of the double feature at the California
Theater, looking up to God
knows what, straining
the galvanized daylight through our fingers
into our half-tranced eyes, checking
the clouds and rooftops, scuffing the soles
of our shoes on the sidewalk
to be sure, with the wind gusts,
that we were still there. . . .

God of absence, God of markers
gone from the fields, God of tail pipes
and mufflers rusting on the roadside,
I pause here to pay respect, to turn
down the page of diminished fact,
to rattle bones so the soul holds on.

But what comfort was there
in the dwarf pine and mesquite,
who was there to pray over the last
mammoth dying under those icy stars
over the Channel Islands? The long ages
moved that far west, coming down
to a last undersized example
adapted to its loneliness, isolated,
one day, by the melting sea. . . .
And the sea so beatific then,
translucent, green as a curling wave,
as a veil Michelangelo draped
over the Sibyl's shoulder
who revealed nothing
on the bright ceiling
of a sorrowful heaven—the way
of the past from which we are meant
to somehow once more draw hope.

We stand in front of the sea again,
everything, it seems, already gone
before us—the consolations, the philosophies
like suits, like old coats to try on
in the Thrift; the religions
like the salvageable shoes shined up—
wing tips and brown & white spectators—

nearly gleaming in the greasy window.
And clouds of dust rising and falling
across the Old West, the Oregon Trail,
El Camino Real.

Still the sky somehow
clearer back there, still at its leisure
to follow a second thought through
the streets with the dying light
block to block, along the dim stations,
past the Carrillo Hotel, the Copper Coffee Pot,
the Fox Arlington. . . . The bruised evening
in the branches of the municipal trees
always at cross-purposes in autumn
as I try to recall anything at all
about what I thought would come—
the salt breeze off the harbor, the little tune
at twilight that softly overcame the red tile roofs,
which I followed west along the sidewalks
where I was first alive, where stars lined up
to arrive with me, home by dark.

About the Author

Christopher Buckley is the chair of the creative writing department at the University of California, Riverside. He has received two grants from the National Endowment for the Arts, most recently for 2001; a Fulbright Award to Yugoslavia; four Pushcart Prizes; and two Pennsylvania Council on the Arts grants and has twice received the Gertrude B. Claytor Memorial Award from the Poetry Society of America. Among his works are the poetry collections *Fall from Grace, Camino Cielo, Dark Matter,* and *Blue Autumn.*